This Gardener's Impossible Dream

"A Not so Green Thumb, (or Why I Took Up Poetry Instead)"

And Other Poems & Translations

by Emery L. Campbell

For Dence —

Poet to poet

Emery L. Campbell

10/20/07

MULTICULTURAL BOOKS (of BC)

"There are many Mansions in Parnassus!"

© EMERY L. CAMPBELL & **MBOOKS** 2005

MULTICULTURAL BOOKS

307 BIRCHWOOD COURT, 6311 GILBERT RD, RICHMOND, BC, V7C 3V7
Tel: (604) 277-3864   E-Mail: jrmbooks@hotmail.com

MBOOKS POETRY SERIES #18
1st print edition—May 2005
ISBN 0-9733301-8-X

Cover image of Confederate Rose used by permission from
      Mr. Jack Sheper of Floridata.com
In-House editor — Joe M. Ruggier
Desk-Top Publishing — Joe M. Ruggier

Library and Archives Canada Cataloguing in Publication

Campbell, Emery L., 1927 -
This Gardener's Impossible Dream: "A Not So Green Thumb, (or Why I Took Up Poetry Instead)": and other poems & translations / by Emery L. Campbell. -- 1st print ed.

(**MULTICULTURAL BOOKS** poetry series; #18)
Also available in electronic format
Includes some translations from the French.
ISBN 0-9733301-8-X

I. Title. II. Series.

PS3603.A4753T44 2005   811'.6   C2005-902396-1

For Hettie

CONTENTS

For Hettie iii
Introduction... vii
Acknowledgments xi

This Garderner's Impossible Dream

Oversight... 2
Walden Farewell 3
Frogs in Earnest 4
Lenore 5
Appallin' Pollen.. 6
A Not So Green Thumb 7
(or Why I Took Up Poetry Instead)....................... 7
The Lion and the Gnat 9
Oh, Dem Golden Slippers..................................... 11
Parting Is Such Seat Sideshow............................. 12
Petrarch Will Circumvolve in His Catacomb I.................. 13
Stock Market on a Roll 14
A Tale of Two Titties.. 15
Genesis.. 17
At Day's End 18
Untidy Battle.. 19
Gone but (Almost) Not Forgotten........................ 20
Help! Pickers Needed 21
The Contest Chairman's Lament 22
Cool Cookout.. 23
Dear Editor... 24
The Oyster and the Litigants................................ 25
Missy Frou-Frou and the Squawk........................ 26
Epigrams 28
Haiku... 30

Kudzu, Kudzu, Go Away; Don't Come Back Another Day
.... 31
Marathon.. 32
Mars Bars Non-Martians from Mars Bars 33
My Ways, Byways.. 34
Through the Looking Glass 35
Sophisticat... 36
Tiger, Tiger, Burning Bite 37
Wedding Photo... 38
The Weigh of All Flesh.. 40
Amazing Grace 42
The Old Cat and the Young Mouse 43
Amerigo Vespucci Probably Got Here First Anyway, So
What's the Big Deal?... 44
Arms and the Mom 45
Aurora's Boring Alice... 46
A Bad Hare's Day.. 47
The Fiftieth of '45 49
Career Woman 50
To the Reader... 51
Parlez-vous ABCDarian?... 53
A Formalist's Credo.. 55
Good News, Bad News... 56
La Fin de la Faim du Fin Gourmet................................. 57
Hettie C 58
Autumn's Song 59
Hit Ain't Never Failed 60
How Do I Loathe You?... 61
I Grow Old, I Grow Old, Must I Shrink from Toxic Mold?
.... 62
Indian Instinct 63
Jumping to Contusions.. 65
A Las Septina de la Tarde 67
The Young Widow.. 69
Liebestod.. 71

Maggie 72
Look! In the Sky! It's a Bird, It's a Plane…No, It's a
Bloomin' Pantoum! 73
Love Ya, Sweetie!.. 74
Maya's First Birthday 75
Pharmaceuticals for Foiling Physical Failings 76
To a Passing Beauty.. 77
Rome's Bells... 78
Witches' Weekend Wind-down............................ 79
There Oughta Be a Law 81
The Joint Is Out of Whack; O Cursed Spite, That Ever Man
Was Born To Set It Right! 83
The Devil's Dictionary 84
Maybelle and Ruthie at Home on the Range 85
Like, Don't Bug Me, Man 86
Culture Clash 87
Don't Buy for Me; Car Too Teeny 89
The Dubliners 90
The Big Bang... 91
Bequests.. 92
Bessie Sees the Wrinkled Dog............................ 93

BIO OF AUTHOR... 94
Afterword.. 95

INTRODUCTION

I HAVE KNOWN Emery Campbell for quite a number of years. Yet, in some ways, he is still an enigma. He lives in Lawrenceville, Georgia, near Atlanta, having retired after a career in the business world. He has a suburban house, a bank account, a beautiful, sensitive, intelligent wife, and unlimited free time.

Why, then, did he not turn to golf or bridge? It is true that both have their critics and detractors. Mark Twain used to say that golf is the quickest way to spoil a good walk As for bridge, if one concentrates enough to guess the cards all the players still have in hand, it is almost impossible for the brain to work normally for the rest of the week.

Emery has turned instead to poetry. We know poetry is the most refined, sophisticated, intense form of literary language. It has been practiced with reverence and enthusiasm since very ancient times. In China and Japan it was always most greatly regarded, followed far behind by prose; essays and novels never rated so high. Greeks and Romans had so little regard for the novel that neither Aristotle nor Horace gave it even a passing glance. Poetry was where the great literary minds developed and contended for honors. Today even a hasty visit to Barnes & Noble or Borders will convince us that the place of poetry in the modern world is much diminished.

And yet...

We know that fashions, in literature as well as in feminine dress, have a way of coming back. Although nobody knows what the future holds in store for poetry, a tradition honored by names such as Homer, Sappho, Shakespeare, Goethe, Poe, Lorca, Neruda, will never disappear. Poetry is to everyday language what dancing is to walking, music to radio static. Perhaps the best is still to come.

Emery Campbell enjoys a clear advantage over many suburban dwellers. In his work and residence abroad and his international travels he has become well acquainted with other cultures, especially French and Hispanic, where poetry is held in higher esteem than here in America. The knowledge of foreign languages makes one more aware of the sound of words, the music and rhythms of language. Emery is familiar with these qualities in the works of La Fontaine and Baudelaire, of Lope de Vega and Lorca.

In modern times, Romantic poets were the ones who attained the utmost influence and prestige in their societies. Byron, Keats, Shelley, Wordsworth, Coleridge, were heroes, legends in their own time. I do not think we can assemble today in the English-speaking world a roster of equal value or influence. These poets chose to write mainly on four lofty themes: Love, Death, Nature, and God. Any other subject paled in comparison with such vast horizons. Other themes, when they appeared in their poetry, would become fused with one or several of the four.

Today we feel less restricted. Furthermore, we may treat the aforementioned dominant subjects with less reverence, with more irony and humor. The danger for Romantic poetry was that it could become pompous and theatrical. Irony and humor are the antidotes to such poisons. Emery knows about these remedies, and makes use of them judiciously and with great results.

Nature is still a subject he loves, yet it is not Nature as seen by Wordsworth or Shelley; it is Nature as seen by Emery Campbell. His mordancy and acute sense of humor treat it in a different way. In this way, he accomplishes a great deed: Nature is no longer overwhelming, but rather familiar, docile, easy to listen to, easy to talk to. This effort may be, at its roots, epic, and yet the results are at the opposite pole from epic poetry.

Who could have guessed that frustration was a true subject for poetry? Nonetheless, if a poem expresses the most important and valuable core of human experience, and if we know, as everyone of us does, that frustration is an essential, permanent reality and possibly resides at the very crux of human experience, how is it that poetry has so often ignored this reality? Emery tries to answer this question.

Ancient Greece offers us clear examples of frustration. Sisyphus, struggling to push a boulder uphill, only to see it tumble down and having to start all over again. Prometheus, chained to a rock, looking at the vulture that devours him time and time again.

Campbell is familiar with similar frustrations, only not in such an epic mode, and this is precisely what makes his poems more striking and understandable for us. In a way, his humor, his irony, make us more aware of the everyday small failures that are our inescapable destiny.

There is a great source of power in poetry, and more generally in literary expression, that critics have often neglected or overlooked: it is the power of a text to compel us, as readers, to identify with the poet's encounters, or perhaps with the literary characters created by the novelist or the playwright. This power is abundantly present in Campbell's poetry, especially in the poems we find in this book. His experiences are our experiences, or perhaps will be in a near future. By identifying with what he tells us, we understand better a part of our life that we had so far neglected to explore. We illuminate, and thus save, an entire range of occurences that we may have found irritating and thus mainly forgettable. He now raises them onto a poetic pedestal, and we can only applaud his success.

Right away we feel better about ourselves: the events in his life are no longer capable of arousing our envy, since they have been followed by such small but repeated failures, and so, for a few moments, we glory in our own cleverness; we may have avoided some (but not all) of his faux pas. Are we really so astute, or is it perhaps that we are simply luckier? In any case, a smile lights the reader's face for a few seconds as he continues discovering Emery's poems. The poet is doubly successful: he sheds light on our life, yet we are placated because it has not been as full of small disasters as his.

Man, as Albert Camus has pointed out, is often unhappy, and then he dies. This is a somber assessment. An American writer, William Saroyan, about to expire in a Paris hospital, remarked that he was bitterly disappointed; he knew all men had to die, but he thought that perhaps in his case a small exception could have been made.

At least I know, and the readers of this book will also soon infer, that Emery Campbell has been unhappy at times, though not often, and furthermore, that he has learned one of the most difficult arts a human being is capable of acquiring: the hard, painful, precarious, bittersweet art of laughing at himself.

I wish I could do the same. Once more, I am starting to envy him all over again...

MANUEL DURÁN
Professor Emeritus, Yale University,
poet, and widely published writer

ACKNOWLEDGMENTS

Grateful acknowledgement is due to the editors of the following periodicals in which some of these poems previously appeared: *Light, The Quarterly of Light Verse; Midwest Poetry Review; Poets' Forum Magazine; Georgia Writers News; Georgia Poetry Society News; SO and SO; manna; Parnassus Literary Journal; Purple Pros* (newsletter of the Southeastern Writers Association); *Romantics Quarterly; HA!; d'Arts; Southern Poetry Review; Calling Earth* (UK); *Harp Strings Poetry Journal*

and anthologies:

Alabama Poetry Society anthology; *Encore* (anthology of the National Federation of State Poetry Societies); *Eternal Portraits; Candlelight; Alalitcom; Reach of Song* (anthology of the Georgia Poetry Society); *Panorama* (anthology of the Utah State Poetry Society); Missouri State Poetry Society anthology; anthology of the Poetry Society of Georgia, Savannah; anthology of the West Virginia Poetry Society; *Fire and Ice; Voices in the Heart; Poet's Voice; 20th Century-Our Times, Our Memories*; Angels Without Wings Foundation anthology; *Where Sunbeams Dance; Manifold* (UK); *Golden Poetry* (KSU); *Seasons of the Heart; Golden Words* (2000 Senior Poet Laureate of U.S.); *Watermarks One* (2004 Senior Poet Laureate of Georgia); *Sunscript* (anthology of Suncoast Writers Conference)

and online:

Sonata/m. e. stubbs poetry journal; The Hyper Texts; Journal of the Blue Planet; Fables.

XII

EMERY L. CAMPBELL

THIS GARDENER'S IMPOSSIBLE DREAM

SELECTED POEMS AND TRANSLATIONS

OVERSIGHT

BLITHE, unwary Willie Wonder,
at the beach he made a blunder;
thought he'd wade in waist-deep water,
went out farther than he oughter.
As the tide swept him away
several friends were heard to say,
"What a shame our little Will
never mastered swimming skill."

WALDEN FAREWELL

IN YOUTHFUL minds the raft we'd set afloat
no longer seemed just logs secured with twine;
our sneakers sloshing full, we'd launched a boat
on which we planned to tame the foaming brine.

We poled the craft through cattails, reeds, and slime,
quite blind to risks, though none of us could swim.
Adventure ruled; ignoring sweat and grime,
our cup of life welled bounteous to the brim.

But such idyllic joys soon ceased to be;
the city drained the pond to make a dump.
Marauding trucks spilled garbage where a tree,
pale green, grew tall--now nothing but a stump.

When "progress" meets perfection and they clash,
to wager on the latter would be rash.

FROGS IN EARNEST

*"Though boys throw stones at frogs in sport, the frogs do
not die in sport, they die in earnest" - Bion, c.325 -255 b.c.*

ALONG the water's edge at Freezee's pond
we'd bash them, trash them any way we could,
and watch them twitch, then hoard the seed they'd
                                        spawned,
scooped up in jars with grass and bits of wood.

The eggs became black commas, wriggling host,
a mass of teeming punctuation marks,
until these bits of life gave up the ghost,
fast-fading, frail, extinguished creature sparks.

At recess time and after school was out
we'd torture Charles whose stutter made it sport,
and I took part, oh shame, a mindless lout,
in savage jibes to see his face contort.

We whooped, ignoring agony and tears,
inflicting wounds to fester all his years.

LENORE

INTERTWINED with the dusky Lenore
I was certain I'd chalk up a score.
I thought, *Now's my chance,*
as I unsheathed my lance,
but she sprang up and quoth, "Nevermore!"

APPALLIN' POLLEN

THE SPRING of '99 will live in shame
as long as pollen counters ply their trade,
for this is when the yellow peril came,
attacked its prey, and left it sorely frayed.

A single snort gives sniffers sneezing spells;
prolonged exposure brings on wracking coughs.
A stuffed up nose suppresses taste and smells:
sustained, untrammeled grief, no ons and offs.

Midwestern refugees who brought along
their shovels used up north for clearing snow
soon realized they hadn't got it wrong:
the scoop serves here to shift the fractious foe.

If you can rid us of the pollen plague,
leave details on my answering machine,
but I want proven means; please, nothing vague.
In meantime, I'm on antihistamine.

A NOT SO GREEN THUMB
(or Why I Took Up Poetry Instead)

NO FLOWERS in the beds
raise up delightful heads
the way they surely should.
A multi-colored fog
in Springhill's catalog;
I'd glory if they would!

White phloxes that I chose
assume a pretty pose,
stand upright, lush, and tall.
Why then do they turn brown,
no blossoms grace their crown,
no gemstones there at all?

My hollyhocks I'd hoped
would thrive, but they just moped,
all ragged and forlorn.
When I was just a kid
they did what mama bid;
now I can only mourn.

My grape vines do not lack
for leaves out there in back;
they flourish, sprawl, and crawl.
But not a single grape
of any kind or shape;
it nearly makes me bawl.

For BLTs I plant
three "Big Boys," then I chant
dread threats to guarantee
tomato fruit will form;
half dozen is the norm.
God's got it in for me.

My realm for one bright spot;

say, weeds that bloom a lot?
I haven't got a clue.
It's time to ditch my trowel,
throw in the muddy towel;
my thumb and I are blue.

THE LION AND THE GNAT[1]

"BEGONE! you petty pest, you less than penny's worth!"
  The lion used such words as these;
  a fiendish midge had plagued his ease.
  At that the gnat declared scorched earth.
"Do you suppose," he asks the beast, "your regal rank
  can frighten me, can make me crawl?
  An ox could best you, to be frank,
  yet I can drive him to the wall."
  The gnat has hardly voiced these facts,
  while circling to survey his meal,
  when, trumpet blaring, he attacks.
  At first he takes his time to wheel,
  then falls upon the lion's neck;
  this makes the king a nervous wreck.
The lion foams and rages, lightning in his eyes.
He bellows; other creatures tremble, run, and hide.
  And this distress, these outraged cries,
  all rise from tricks a gnat has tried.
The puny gnat torments the king in every wise.
At times he bites his back, and then he pricks his snout;
  he buzzes up his nose, then out.
The lion's astronomic rage inspires awe.
Unseen, the demon triumphs, and he laughs to view
the maddened beast who's sparing neither tooth nor claw
in wild contortions, even shedding blood as, through
his anguish, he does grievous damage to his skin.
He whips his tail with frantic force from side to side
and beats the blameless air. His fury does him in
at last, fatigues him, brings him down; he's mortified.
The bully bug pulls back with glory written large
and trumpets triumph much as he'd proclaimed the
                                        charge.
He flits about and cries,"I won!" but on the way
    he's tangled in a spider's snare;
    once victor, now he too is prey.

---

[1] Translated from the fable "*Le lion et le moucheron*" by Jean de La Fontaine, 1621- 1695.

What useful lesson can we learn from this affair?
I'll name you two: the first is that among our foes
the ones that we must fear the most are often those
of smallest size. The other: whom great peril spares
    can die from tumbling down the stairs.

OH, DEM GOLDEN SLIPPERS

BANANAS, UGH! They're not what I'd call treats,
and when they're overripe they make me sick.
I'm mostly game for any kind of eats,
but look: this slippery fruit and I don't click.

Bananas, even green ones, in the fridge
for more than just a couple overnights
turn dark and mushy, only good to squidge.
The thought of eating one gives me the frights.

Bananas, sliced, arrayed on Choco Pops,
then drowned with milk and sugar substitute:
clear grounds for grievance. Quickly, call the cops!
They're trained to chuck 'em down the garbage chute.

Bananas, yellow, black, or brown, or green
are my ideal first choice for shoat cuisine.

Emery L. Campbell

PARTING IS SUCH SEAT SIDESHOW

I BEND; the stresses, vengeful Huns,
they sunder seam—my trousers split,
revealing bare rear bumper buns;
I blush all reddish over it.

Six Girl Scouts squeal, their leader swoons:
how could the Fates be so unkind?
It's eventide; a pallid moon's
highlighting my exposed behind.

Retreat's in order, back away.
Oh no! They're dialing 911.
If cops come there'll be hell to pay
before this episode is done.

The moral: let the penny lie.
Do not be tempted; pass on by.

PETRARCH WILL CIRCUMVOLVE IN HIS CATACOMB I

FROWN NOW, brown cow, thou fount of frothy foam!
What other tumid phrases can I milk
from idle ruminations of that ilk
before they haul me howling to a home?
Dare I, for laughs, provoke a purists' storm
by forging faulty sonnet lines this way,
abusing old Petrarca's *declassé*
yet passing popular poetic form?

I'm sorely tempted; it's the fool in me.
I'll blame on rank senectitude
the fiery fallout that is bound to come.
This flagrant lack of tact that ought to be,
instead, the soul of righteous rectitude
intrigues me more than keeping mum.

STOCK MARKET ON A ROLL

I TOOK my bread out of a box,
invested it in bakery stocks.

Inflation fears swell in the east,
while loaves are formed and pans are greased.

I'll know that I have bought a prize
when needed dough begins to rise.

A TALE OF TWO TITTIES

ATOP A list of long-mistaken lore
lies Lil's illicit, legendary lilt,
a lyric launching very little more
than loony, laugh-provoking, lustful guilt.

The tale it tells is close to being true,
although, from talk with those who took the time
to tally tacit tidbits tagged taboo,
the truth turns out too tame to be a crime.

In short, she sheds her shirt, thus shows her shape.
No shielding shades are shut as Lili primps.
The sheriff sees, is shocked, and stands agape,
for Lili's treasures are no shrinking shrimps.

Some crackers crowd around 'mid cameras' clicks.
The cop, concerned that custom's compromised,
corrals the crush and kindly calms the chick's
confusion, calls her cancan ill-advised.

He shares that she should shelve her fear of shame.
He'll shroud the case to give the sylph a chance:
no spot shall ever shine upon her name.
The shook-up sheila shoots the cop a glance.

She fears she's falling for the fellow fast,
for finer face and form she's never found.
The cop's affected, too, and thinks, 'At last
I find that I feel free, now she's around,

the woman whom I'll ask to be my wife.'
The way they waltz and woo works wondrous well.
Their world is wide; they want to weld for life
and wish without delay a wedding bell.

The duo lovey-doves. The day dawns damp
but does not daunt the dude who claims his prize.
That night his bride disports it like a vamp,
though past exposure spares him some surprise.

GENESIS

DEEP NIGHT gives way to lustrous glint of gold.
Winged sylvan songsters loose exultant peals.
Dew droplets gleam; oh! wondrous to behold.
Glimpsed through the trees, despairing crescent steals

away to hide as zephyrs fresh and pure,
air redolent of pine and waking earth
announce with gentle breath a day *en fleur*,
a promise of excitement and rebirth.

Slow luminescence gilds the eastern sky:
a curtain rising with Apollo's aid,
while two reclusive possums scurry by
to seek their secret lair in forest's shade.

An aching splendor swells each dawn's array
as sunbeams wake and venture out to play.

AT DAY'S END[2]

DEMENTED under pallid light,
life rushes, writhes, kicks legs up high,
a shameless squaller, uncontrite.
Thus, when enticing night comes nigh,

relieving even day-long fast,
effacing even shame's disgrace,
the Poet murmurs low: "At last!
My spirit and my bones embrace

the welcome prospect of a rest.
My heart's so full of dismal dreams,
I'll lie supine, and 'round my breast,

O cooling shades whose freshness teems,
I'll drape your folds whence bracing streams
of grace will flow as your bequest."

---

[2] Translated from the poem "*Fin de la journée*" from *Les fleurs du mal* by Charles Baudelaire (1821-1867).

UNTIDY BATTLE

BRAVE Prince Valiant stood facing the horde;
unafraid, he unsheathed his broad sword.
He slashed right and left,
not a Hun was uncleft;
made a mess that he truly deplored.

GONE BUT (ALMOST) NOT FORGOTTEN

WHENEVER will my heart get over this?
Good lord! How can I hope to keep my grip?
It's not as if another's proffered kiss
could substitute; it wouldn't have the zip.

The ardor that we shared has gone astray.
I never could have possibly foreseen
that she'd so blithely throw our love away
in circumstances so unfair and mean,

thus wrenching from my breast winged Cupid's dart.
Oh, how it hurts, so deeply I am cleft;
it's tearing me to shreds. But wait! My heart
has skipped a beat. That redhead on the left,

just coming in the door. Jeez, what a bod!
"How 'bout it, honey? Wanna promenade?"

HELP! PICKERS NEEDED

THE FIG tree that I planted late last fall
sure took its own sweet time to wake this spring,
but then at last a bud appeared, so small
I really had to squint to see the thing.

I checked its progress as the days went by.
Before I knew it more had come in view,
then tender leaves unfurled to greet the eye,
and baby figlets, more than just a few.

The way the harvest's grown has forced my hand.
I've had to order crates to hold the crops
and line up contract deals throughout the land
with truckers, supermarkets, gourmet shops.

Who knew the tree would land for me a gig
as fruitdom's foremost fancy fig bigwig?

THE CONTEST CHAIRMAN'S LAMENT

Dear Entrant,

BEST THANKS for sending me your droll pantoum;
the postman dropped it in my box today.
The problem is to know what to assume
regarding your intentions; you don't say.

The postman dropped it in my box today
without the fee, nor was the contest named.
What your intentions are you do not say.
If I am puzzled, then I can't be blamed.

You sent no fee; the contest wasn't named.
I asked myself what action I should take.
It puzzled me; I feared I would be blamed.
At last I chose the proper move to make.

I settled on the action I should take:
I'd send you guidelines so you'd know the form.
It surely was the move that I should make;
then you could fit your entry to the norm.

Enclosed to guide your steps you have the form.
Please let me know just what I should assume
so I can match your entry with the norm
and thank you once again for your pantoum.

Pantoumly (more or less) yours,

The Contest Chairman

COOL COOKOUT

TO THOSE whose collars cover crimson skin,
a barbecue's a dented pickup truck,
careening, filled with rowdy mountain kin
well oiled with beer and primed to run amok.

It's smoky, dripping ribs, and sweaty brows,
thick Brunswick stew, grilled corn, and greasy lips,
a plate of beans, a battle flag to rouse
a rebel yell, bib overalls, 'shine sips.

But look who's here today: you'll be amazed.
Those gathered 'round the grill are quite genteel;
each downs his drink with little finger raised,
ingests, but with restraint, his tasty meal.

What awesome essence does this group comprise?
Are some among them blessed with special traits
beyond their charm and bright, seductive eyes,
perhaps so skilled that future fame awaits?

The answer's plain, I need inquire no more:
the sacred p-word springs at once to mind.
They're Poets, wily wordsmiths to the core,
acclaimed, distinguished, widely wined and dined.

So that explains the elevated vein:
a bards' bucolic banquet in the 'burbs.
We've steaks and burgers, chips, the bread's whole-grain,
the salad's drenched with olive oil and herbs.

Recite a verse or two to set the tone,
then fill your plate with white-neck barbecue.
The meat will be more tender on the bone
when sampled with iambic derring-do.

DEAR EDITOR

HERE, CHOSEN from my new pomes, one:
I wove it with my brow all knitted.
A sure lock as to rhyme, homespun,
and meter, too; my teeth I gritted.

As is my wont, on having done
my level best, I then respited.
I'll wait and pray you'll think it fun,
that in your mag it can be fitted.

Ever hopefully yours,

T. H. Ebard, Esq.

THE OYSTER AND THE LITIGANTS[3]

A PAIR of pilgrims on the beach one day
espied an oyster which the waves had just
washed up. They eyed it, pointed where it lay;

but who should eat it roused in them distrust.
One pilgrim stooped at once to snatch the snack;
the other stopped him. "Wait; we must decide
    on who will get to toss it back.
The one who was the first to have descried
the find will gulp it down; his mate may pout."

    "If that's how we're to sort this out,"
replies his friend, "I have good eyes, thank God."
    "My eyesight, too, is far from flawed,"
the other says, "I saw it first, no fraud."
"I smelled it first, so I should get the nod."
    While this dispute was taking place,
a judge arrived to whom the two deferred.
He gravely ate the treat, their pleas unheard.
    The two men watched him, face to face.
The meal complete, he said with regal grace:

"Look here, the court awards you each a shell,
no charge. Now go in peace to where you dwell.
Consider what a court case costs these days;
just think what little's left to many folks;
you'll see that I'm the one the process pays,
while litigants become the butt of jokes."

---

[3] Translated from the fable "*L'huître et les plaideurs*" by Jean de La Fontaine (1621-1695).

MISSY FROU-FROU AND THE SQUAWK

A SCARY band of witches in their coven
were playing tapes by Ludwig van Beethoven,
though one cried, "I like prom toots by Frank Schubert!"
A carefree, shapely, pert, assured, and cute flirt,
she wore her dresses mini length, though jet black,
with less than decent coverage of her bare back.

The music notes inspired Missy Frou-Frou,
for that's the nifty nickname she'd laid claim to,
to rise above her compeers on a broomstick;
she wanted them to see she was a cool chick.
She didn't know a waltz from a sonata,
but of resounding brass she had a lotta.

She really has appeal, thought Squawker Squigman,
who ranked among the underworld's bigwig-men.
Said he, "Her sexy swoopings make me dizzy."
Said she, "He ain't a bad nogoodnik, izzy?"
It seemed a romance was to be expected;
two bods like that just had to get connected.

The Squawk employed a helicopter pilot,
a real gung-ho, ex-military zealot,
to fly his private city-hopper chopper
whenever Mr. Big-Boss found it proper.
It didn't take him long to round up witchy;
the Squawker had it done 'cause he got itchy.

Ace schlepped 'er to the latter as he oughter.
Said he to him, "As ordered, I have brought 'er."
The capo had a good close look at Frou-Frou,
and right away he knew he loved her beaucoup.
Before the day was out he'd popped the question:
to wed ASAP was his suggestion.

The diamond ring he gave her sparkled brightly.
Her cleavage claimed his thoughts both day and nightly.
Miss Frou-Frou swelled with pride, her bust near bust-out;

she, too, could hardly wait to let her lust out.
They tied the knot, and with the priest's permission,
the two sucked face; it's what they'd both been wishin'.

Within a week a bun was in the oven;
it's hard to fantasize such frenzied lovin'.
From that day on they had an offspring yearly,
first boys, then girls in turn, and loved them dearly.
The Squawk gave up his mobbing, Frou her witching,
devoted all their time to soothe the itching.

And so they lived and loved forever after
'mid kids and pets, exuberance and laughter.
The point? To keep your bearing bold, not boring,
mix crime and witchy cocktails; go on pouring."

EPIGRAMS[4]

HI DIDDLE Diddle, the Fat 'round the Middle

CRIPPLING plaque from fast food grows.
Next stop: cemetery rows.

FIRST Sinus Spring (Not Robins)

A GREENING spring without the pollen
would surely be much more enthrallin'.

PUNCHIN' Judy

HOW FAR, I wonder, can I go
before her left jab lays me low.

THE BIBLE Tells Me So

SIN'S WAGES may indeed be death—
unless that's just a shibboleth.

HERE Today, Gone Tomorrow

LOVE IS longing,
love's belonging,
till one's lover
runs for cover.

IN VINO Veritas

STONED, beneath the table, mumbled "Waiter,
better leave cigars and port till later."

FRUITY Beauty

Lovely Rose would smell much sweeter
if she weren't a garlic eater.

---

[4] Short, pithy, comic or satiric poems.

UNWORTHY Wordsmith

I'VE ALWAYS yearned to be a writer;
too bad I'm not a few shades brighter.

HAIKU

THUNDER shakes the sky
loosens waiting water drops
waiting water drops

KUDZU, KUDZU, GO AWAY; DON'T COME BACK ANOTHER DAY

WE HAVE a plague, a brawling, sprawling weed,
a vile, rapacious, rampant, grasping foe.
Extensive education's what we need
to smite this evil scourge a telling blow.

The curse of roadside berms and woodlands, too,
the vines exist in great variety:
K. strangulatus, born of witches' brew,
exceeds them all in notoriety.

I feel we must raise high a scarlet flag
to publicize the nature of the beast.
Here, take these packs; in each I've sealed and tagged
ten kudzu seeds indicted by a priest.

First study them, then crush them with a crash
and fling the fractured fragments in the trash.

MARATHON

ON MY BLISTERED feet kept pounding
struggling strides no longer bounding
swarming motes formed clouds about me
scourge I feared would surely rout me
tortured chest that stabs were wracking
gasping breath so sorely lacking
would not let my rhythm alter
would not stumble retch or falter
tortured legs infirm and leaden
face to face with armageddon
then at last the finish nearing
fuddled thinking started clearing
dug down deep to go on churning
kept the crippled cog wheels turning
strained to persevere at plumbing
my reserves though pain was numbing
suddenly the tape before me
reeling lunged although it tore me
staggered three more steps and tumbled
tried to rise as crowd roars rumbled
heard my name as thousands chanted
stood at last feet firmly planted

I had done it I had won it
I had won it I had won it

MARS BARS NON-MARTIANS FROM MARS BARS

OUR TRIP began with thunderous, flaming heat.
Some seven months of pap in plastic tubes
was all they let us bring along to eat;
no salted nuts, no Cokes with frozen cubes.

As touchdown neared the retros loosed their thrust;
the cabin jerked and shook, all huff and puff.
The rocket's blast stirred up a swirl of dust;
we'd heard the place was powdered with the stuff.

At last debarked, we thought, 'Let's have some drinks.
With local carbonation. On the rocks.'
But no, the spiteful little three-eyed finks
had sealed the taverns' doors with fool-proof locks.

The signs above the entries made it clear:
"No geeks from space will ever quaff our beer."

MY WAYS, BYWAYS[5]

ADRIFT down country lanes, my fists through pocket
                                                holes,
my easy, lived-in topcoat looking far from new,
I'd stroll beneath the heavens, faithful, Muse! to you.
What splendid loves were mine: romantic, matchless
                                                roles!

My sole remaining trousers had a gaping tear.
Tom Thumb, vague dreamer, as I rambled I would pluck
my rhymes. Above, my stars swished soft and I,
                                                awestruck,
would lie in earthbound thrall beneath the sky's Great
                                                Bear

and heed their call. I listened there, beside the road,
those lovely, fresh September eves as dewdrops glowed
upon my brow like tonic wine to spur my art.

Amid fantastic shades I'd fashion rhymes and use
elastic, tautened laces of my stricken shoes
to strum like lyre strings, one foot drawn near my heart!

---

[5] Translated from the poem "*Ma bohême*" by Arthur Rimbaud (1854-1891).

THROUGH THE LOOKING GLASS

MY EARLY life had limited frontiers,
constrained by meager means within a land
of baseball, hot dogs, Walgreen's, high school proms,
where mostly English speech is what one hears.
I'd never been where great cathedrals stand,
the Duomos, Chartres, Ulm, the Notre Dames.

A scholarship to France unveiled my eyes
to narrow, cobbled streets, to broader skies.

Imagine if you can the thrill I felt
discovering the splendid Tuileries,
enraptured by the hand that I'd been dealt;
the Louvre glimpsed through stately chestnut trees;
my first croissant. I thought my heart would melt.
A new world's door swung wide; I'd found the keys.

SOPHISTICAT

I'VE A BROWN, black, and white spotted kitty
with a character charming and witty.
When I say to him, "Friend,
you just don't comprehend,"
with a shrug he responds, "More's the pity."

TIGER, TIGER, BURNING BITE

I HOLD in hand the tiger's tooth,
extracted from my bottom.
He gnawed me, fickle cut, forsooth;
zoo-keepers came and got 'im.

I'd had him since he was a cub,
I'd nursed him with a bottle,
but now I'm naught to him but grub,
a morsel epiglottal.

It pains me where I'd like to sit;
his actions smack of treason,
though what I fed him, I'll admit,
could well have been the reason.

Two cans of kitty food most days
won't sate a tiger's hunger,
above all when the beast of prey's
not getting any younger.

WEDDING PHOTO

THEY TAKE a bow, sun-dappled bower, proud by rustic
                                                    rail;
their gaze off-center, flowing flowers. Handsome groom in
                                                    tux,
soup-strainer spruce. His prize resplendent, snowy gown
                                              and tail.
The rite, her knight. The bills will come; her dad will
                                        pay the bucks.

The cake is next. She nicely slices; layers, gooey glop.
It's custom-made, art, sculpted, icing, not a crumb amiss;
a pyramid, it towers skyward, two wee bods on top.
Bride stuffs her mouth, then turns to husband, plants a
                                              sticky kiss.

String band tunes up, starts sawing fiddles, dancers take
                                              the floor;
our couple's there, right in the middle, whirling, wedding
                                              waltz.
The day wears on, a frightful funfest, booze-fed
                                        Terpsichore.
In fact, too much, some tumble, sodden; calls for smelling
                                              salts.

At dusk the duo on display, a great deal worse for wear,
takes stock. Her gown's in disarray, stained, torn. Her
                                        leg is hurt
by hubby's clumsy hoof; he'd reared and stumbled on a
                                              chair.
His tie's askew, his visage wan; there's lipstick on his shirt.

They take their leave with waves and tears to drive to
                                        their hotel.
The guests still standing give a cheer, tie cans and shoes
                                        behind.
Poor bridal pair, they're slightly greenish, pale and quite
                                        unwell.

They slump in bed. Embrace? Some other time; they're
                                                not inclined.

******

One snap is worth a thousand phrases, per the rationale,
but clearly it, in many cases, may not tell it all.

THE WEIGH OF ALL FLESH[6]

YOU MAKE me queasy, you'll have to change;
you've just got to disdain such big meals,
give up fries that you love, cut desserts to just one.
You must believe me; I want to see the slim girl I once
                                              knew,
not one whose dress bursts when she dines.
I'm sick when your chewings accrue.
You've got to make it happen, you must arrange
to savor your meals with less zeal,
to gaze through bake shop windows, looking down at their
                                              buns
without touching a crumb,
not running around trying apple pie, too,
as if nothing repressed you at all;
shun what you are tempted to do..

Don't eat with glee, my dear Tina,
try to be less contrary—don't say you can't,
less unmindful of my contention
that large candy bars are what you must bar.

Try not to gain, scorn the people
who snack; skip your turn. Sign up as a member
of Thinning Solutions, eat Weight Watchers rations,
stop bingeing forever, my once-tiny Tina,
quit gorging forever, become Mini-Tina,
not a news story, gracing a coffin,
the saddest of stories, gracing a coffin.

Don't try more brie, bulging Tina,
in truth I can hardly lift you.
All through your child days, your teenage ferments,
recall your promise: no self-indulgence.
Start every forenoon, play the game,
don't ever let cravings win
though you once felt big lunches were all you desired.

---

[6] a parody of "Don't Cry for Me, Argentina"

Fats in profusion are indeed the pollution they're touted
to be.
The cure lies in you; it's a crime
ingesting to such a degree.

You will walk with a crutch for sure if you don't heed
what I say to you.
All it takes is to look in the mirror to see that my words
are true.

AMAZING GRACE
(An acrostic)

AN INEFFECTIVE bumbler as a child,
Miss Gracie couldn't even tie her shoes.
A brat by nature, she was rather wild;
zoo visits she adored...to see the gnus.
In spite of such an inauspicious start,
no runner ever trained as hard as she.
Gargantuan were her efforts; she had heart.
Gosh, even fleet gazelles trailed whirlwind G.
Relentless, blessed with overwhelming speed;
a blur was all one saw—no other trace.
Confounding skeptics all, she did the deed:
exceeded sound, then light. Amazing, Grace!

THE OLD CAT AND THE YOUNG MOUSE[7]

AN ARTLESS mouse, too young to know where logic lay
Had hoped that he could hold a grown-up cat at bay
By choosing certain reasoned concepts to espouse;
   "I beg you, let me live: a mouse
   As small as I and hardly in the way
   Is surely not a cause to grouse.
   To owner, wife, and all their house,
   Who'd miss the little I should eat?
   A crumb that falls upon their blouse
   Or tiny nut is all I need.
Right now I'm thin; if you would condescend to wait
I'll serve to keep your children in a well-fed state."
'Twas thus the mouse addressed the cat who held him
                      firm.
   The other said, "You're wrong, you worm.
Is it to me that one should voice such thoughts as these?
As well you importune the deafened with your pleas.
A cat, and old at that, to let you off? Absurd!
   Our laws are clear: go meet your fate
   Go die at once, and at the gate
   The keepers will not heed a word.
My children will not lack for food to fill their plate."
   He kept his word. As for my tale,
Here present is the moral that best fits the case:
A youth deludes himself; he takes up any chase.
   To age all calls for grace will fail.

---

[7] Translated from the fable "*Le vieux chat et la jeune souris*" by Jean de
La Fontaine (1621-1695).

AMERIGO VESPUCCI PROBABLY GOT HERE FIRST ANYWAY, SO WHAT'S THE BIG DEAL?

COLUMBUS sailed the ocean blue
in fourteen hundred ninety two.

He sailed across the deep blue sea
in fourteen hundred ninety three.

The man from Europe cracked the door
in fourteen hundred ninety four.

There was no telecasting live
in fourteen hundred ninety five.

He got his navigation fix
in fourteen hundred ninety-six.

When winds were strong, Cap Chris thanked Heaven
in fourteen hundred ninety seven.

There's some debate about the date
of fourteen hundred ninety eight.

He ploughed through surging waves of brine
in fourteen hundred ninety-nine.

No wonder it's so hard to teach
exactly when he reached the beach!

ARMS AND THE MOM

A MOTHER saddled heavily with more than she could
shoulder
had come to fear the end was near unless she found relief.
With dirty diapers piling up, the fragrance would enfold
'er;
to tired mum a smeary bum brought blues beyond belief.

She also had to cook and clean. What toil! She tried to
blot it.
She'd quite despaired of handling all the tasks still left to
do.
She dreamt of having one more arm, and then one day
she got it!
Yep, down she glanced and counted three where once
she'd had but two.

At first it seemed an oddity; stunned Mizzes turned back,
staring,
but then they saw utility in how it helped her cope,
for these were burdens other women also had been
sharing.
They begged to know her secret; having three, too, was
their hope.

The thing caught on like wildfire; soon all moms were so
constructed.
What luck! The extra arm allowed more work to be
conducted.

AURORA'S BORING ALICE

OH, NOTABLE for lobos' cries,
for bear-infested lanes,
for temps of minus ten degrees,
and spates of freezing rains,

Alaskaland! Alaskaland!
Seals bolt fresh fish on thee!
One strolls thy woods
with snug rainhoods
and flees each falling tree.

A BAD HARE'S DAY
(A glose)

"THE TURTLE lives 'twixt plated decks
which practically conceal its sex.
I think it clever of the turtle
in such a fix to be so fertile."[8]

A turtle racing with a hare
was losing badly till he saw
that brother rabbit took no care
to mull if he could safely dare
recline to ease a painful paw.
He'd had too many lengthy treks;
indeed, his foot was worn quite raw.
He stretched out on a bed of straw
and thus incurred a heavy hex.
Though turtle lived 'twixt plated decks,

a heavy load to drag along,
he nonetheless kept plodding, drawn
by his belief he wasn't wrong
to seek success. His legs were strong;
true, speed he lacked, but he had brawn—
he manifested muscle flex—
and so he vowed to carry on
(though not, of course, as did Don Juan,
for turtles' love is quite complex;
they practically conceal their sex).

The rabbit meanwhile lay asleep,
a slumped, deep breathing, furry mound,
unmindful how the hours could leap,
no clock to blurt a waking beep,
unconscious on the straw he'd found.
His foe could not be said to hurtle,
but all the same he covered ground,
stepped soft, took care to make no sound;

---

[8] From "Hard Times" by Ogden Nash.

just ten more yards—the final hurdle.
All hail triumphant, clever turtle!

At last the hare jumped up, awake,
saw slowpoke was so far ahead—
near out of sight, for goodness sake!
He leapt to try to overtake
his rival. In despair he sped,
but 'twas too late. In meantime, Myrtle,
our hero's wife, with kids he'd bred,
stood waiting with their arms outspread
to cheer him on and to engirdle
their Papa, eminently fertile.

THE FIFTIETH OF '45

*(Written on the fiftieth anniversary of the graduation of the
Monroe, WI, High School class of 1945)*

THE WINNOWING of time has played its role;
our ranks are thinning slowly year by year.
I felt it was their due that we extol
our former classmates now no longer here.

Their faces, eyes, and spirits once were bright,
their youth and vigor welled and overflowed,
but since, on wings of death they've taken flight
and rest now in their ultimate abode.

Turn back your thoughts to days when we were young,
before these fifty years had scurried by,
and for a time let them abide among
the shades of vanished friends from Monroe High.

A silence in their honor we'll allot
and wonder...that we live...and they do not.

CAREER WOMAN

A LATE-NIGHT sales meeting, then Hannah
rushed home to fry eggs in a pan-a.
She blackened them both
at which the lass quoth,
"Oh well, I'll just open a can-a."

To the Reader[9]

SHEER folly, errors, sin, tight-fisted greed
engross our spirits, bait our spineless clay.
Our nice remorse's hunger we allay
as beggars nourish well their vermin's need.

Our sins are stubborn, our contrition feigned,
confessions stir our guilt; we pay a price,
yet we regain bad pathways in a trice,
believing cut-rate tears leave us unstained.

On evil's pillow, Satan, three times great,
is he who slowly lulls enchanted souls
and soon our tempered, steel-like wills, our goals,
that learned chemist will eliminate.

The Devil holds the strings that make us dance;
repugnant objects lure us with false charms.
Descending daily closer to Hell's arms,
we pass, detached, through stinking gloom's expanse.

Like pauper profligates who mouth and kiss
the martyred breasts of ancient prostitutes,
we steal in passing pleasures destitute
and squeeze them hard to plumb our lust's abyss.

A seething mass of parasites distends
our brain, base Demons staging drinking bouts,
and when we breathe, the unseen Reaper spouts
complaints in muffled tones as he descends.

If rape, the dagger, poison, searing flame,
have not yet cross-stitched with their droll motifs
the vapid canvas of our sad fate's grief,
it's that our soul does not bear valor's name.

---

[9] Translated from the poem "*Au lecteur*" from *Les fleurs du mal* by
Charles Baudelaire (1821-1867).

But there among the jackals, panthers, hounds,
the serpents, spiders, vultures, baleful apes,
the yapping, howling, grunting monster shapes,
the zoo where all our breeds of vice abound,

there's one more foul, more ugly, meaner still,
although he hardly moves or spawns great cries,
who'd gladly make of earth a wrecker's prize
and in his maw would slurp the world as swill.

It's Boredom!--eyes awash, the grudging tear,
he dreams of gallows while he smokes his pipe.
You, reader, know this dainty monster type,
--deceitful reader—fellow man—my peer!

PARLEZ-VOUS ABCDARIAN?

(A poem in which the first letters of all 26 lines are arranged in alphabetical order from A to Z.)

A GENTLE rain that's fallen through the night,
by virtue of its boon to plants and lawn
could ease at last our flowers' frightful plight,
disastrous due to drought's too lengthy spawn.

Enough of flora's anguished, wilting plea!
For much too long we've watched as beauty dies.
Gardenias' nectar sought by honeybee
has disappeared, and roses agonize.

It's Satan's work that must be overcome.
Jehovah will assist to calm our fears;
keep faith, and we shall hear salvation's drum.
Look first to Him; give thanks as rescue nears.

Maltreated, withered blooms will wake and bear
new petals, gaining strength as raindrops fall
on blighted earth; it's clear the Lord does care.
Perfume of roses soon will greet us all.

Quite dreadful are the stresses plants must face
regarding twists and turns that nature makes.
Soft raindrops now will be their saving grace;
they'll profit from whatever form it takes.

Until milieus evolve quite free of drought,
vicissitudes will plague plants, as you see.
Without sufficient water, there's no doubt
xerophilous[10] is what they need to be.

****

You're nearly home. Hang in there, reader friend.
Zucchini! There, thank God, at last an end!

---

[10] Of plants or animals adapted for growing or living in dry surroundings.

FISHIE CATCHIE, SOFTLY, SOFTLY

*(A poem in which the first letters of all 26 lines are
arranged in reverse alphabetical order from Z to A)*

ZARGANA[11] suits the Greeks, their favorite dish
you see, but it's just not my cup of tea:
X-rated, boring, though I do like fish,
well grilled and seasoned, with a chilled Chablis.

Vacations I devote, come rain or drought,
untutored though I am with hook and line,
to catching, if I can, a wily trout.
Sabbaticals for me mean rise and shine

regardless of the season, rod in hand.
Quite likely I shall find myself a spot,
perhaps along a sylvan stretch of sand
on brooklet's bank, in hip boots I have bought.

Not knowing where my prey lies hidden, I
might flick my fly in sparkling pools of glass-
like water formed where eddies still. If my
keen eyesight spots a ripple where the grass

just casts a shadow on the water's edge,
I'll slowly lift the rod to tantalize,
high-strung, beneath his underwater ledge,
God's beauty, Mister Trout. If he should rise

from where he lurks, perhaps he'll take the bait
enabling me to win. The thought, once aired,
does bring to mind the countless times I'd wait,
content to hope against all odds that there'd

be trout filets at dinnertime to grace
a plate at every hungry diner's place.

---

[11] A gar-like fish caught in waters off the coast of Greece.

A FORMALIST'S CREDO

I TRY TO plant my feet upon the page
in such a way that gist and form are served
in roughly equal measure, to assuage
my purist bent that's oftentimes unnerved

by wildly twisted meter in the grip
of some deluded view that rules don't count.
An iamb's not a concept one can skip
en route to scale a formal poem's mount.

There are, we know, iconoclasts who say
that guidelines, codes, and laws exist to break,
that black is white or sundry shades of gray,
and those who claim there's not a lot at stake.

Well, as for me, I choose the formal route.
What else did you expect from this old coot?

GOOD NEWS, BAD NEWS

OF MIGHTY forces deemed eclectic,
the ones whose clout we most respect,
near topping all's high-tech electric;
can cause convulsions if unchecked.

Thus cables, toasters, plugs are shielded
to keep crisp current close at heel;
on flick of switch full power's wielded,
but do beware! Dire danger's real.

Belle Bluehair sits in coiffeur's chamber,
her dryer hums, then sudden flame!
Before her time, yet curtains claimed her;
was not her fault, a frying shame.

Great progress often comes with downers;
base, wretched dirty tricks abound.
I s'pose it's true. Well, hang the frowners;
just plug it in…but mind the ground!

LA FIN DE LA FAIM DU FIN GOURMET[12]

HE'S SAVORED each delicious bite, each bit
of tender, nicely-seasoned rack of lamb,
but now this most outrageous slight, to wit,
a sad soufflé not worth a tinker's damn,

is proffered as dessert. How less than grand!
Mere gourmandise alone does not accord
the right to deal gauche host a reprimand;
yet, such injustice cannot be ignored.

Our epicure surveys the scene anew.
His glass of wine's there on the field of play.
With studied stealth he plays it mean. Oops! Ooh!
The goblet's spilled to everyone's dismay.

Good grief! Dessert afloat in muscatel!
And not a single serving left? What hell…

---

[12] The keen gourmet loses his appetite

HETTIE C
(A sette bello)

HER NAME in fact is really Henriette,
except, that tag you may as well forget.
The one that she prefers gives me a thrill;
to mouth it makes the ache inside me still.
Incredibly
entrancing, wondrous music, do re mi,
consumes my heart when hearing Hettie C.

AUTUMN'S SONG[13]

LONG sobs begin
from violins
of autumn.
They pierce my heart;
their anguished art
leaves me numb.

Throat choked with grief,
pale, when brief
hours knell
I call to mind
days left behind,
and tears well.

I'm borne away
on winds of prey—
fitful thieves—
whirl right, drift left,
like sere, bereft
dead leaves.

---

[13] Translated from the poem "*Chanson d'automne*" by Paul Verlaine (1844-1896).

HIT AIN'T NEVER FAILED

SUMMER'S a'comin' on,
loud sing gol' durn.
Sun's a'blastin' down our necks,
ain't no place left that's cool,
sing gol' durn.

Blisterin' drought, grass bin kilt,
blight's hit mah yard.
Flamin' heat wave, ban on warter,
dang it, sing gol' dang.

Gol' dang, gol' dang,
Ah'm bugged Ah am, gol' dang,
ain't got no breeze or rain.
Sing gol' dang, dang, sing gol' dang,
sing gol' dang, yell gol' damn,
DAMN!

(With apologies to Ezra Pound)

HOW DO I LOATHE YOU?

HOW DO I loathe you? With the laser ray
I'll sear you to the depth the shaft will slice
in long-held beam. Indeed, I'll do it twice
to end your being; what an ideal way!
I loathe you truly. Ever on display,
your visage makes me sick as death, the price
of years in torment. Nothing will suffice
save seeing you cut down; I'll make you pay.

I loathe you all the more that you abuse
my core beliefs, deep-felt. Defilement, blows,
the threats you loose when nether-bound on booze,
your wanton acts base infamy expose.
For tears but never smiles I gladly choose
to fix on your demise—and my repose.

(With apologies to E. B. Browning)

"Toxic varieties of mold, or fungus, have joined radon, carbon monoxide, and lead on the list of potentially hazardous substances in the home. The three molds most apt to create health problems are stachybotrys, aspergillus, and penicillium (the same mold that makes the antibiotic)."
Atlanta Constitution Health Watch, October 28, 1997.

I GROW OLD, I GROW OLD, MUST I SHRINK FROM TOXIC MOLD?

I'VE LIVED my life, as have so many men,
with scarce attention paid to Rn fear.
I've sniffed in vain for CO now and then,
and Pb's never put me off my beer.

But now it seems those streaks on shower stalls
could well be ominous encroaching tongues
of toxic mold; the thought alone appalls.
They say the bane can lead to bleeding lungs!

It could be poison penicillium,
or stalking stachybotrys on the prowl.
Atrocious aspergillus might become
the cause of dire disarray most foul.

For God's sake, let such revelations cease
so I can pass my days and nights in peace.

INDIAN INSTINCT

ONE AUTUMN members of an Indian tribe
approached their newly-chosen chief to know
if he'd consult the gods and then describe
how cold the coming winter winds would blow.

The product of our modern age, the chief
had never learned the ancient secrets, so
he feared that he would only come to grief
by trying on his own to be a pro.

To play it safe, he said they could expect
the coming season would be very cold,
so they had better hasten to collect
a lot of wood. They did as they were told.

The leader, being blessed from birth with smarts,
conceived a plan so he would know for sure.
He phoned the weather service. "Check your charts.
In view of all your data, what is your

prediction of how cold it's going to be
next winter." They replied, "You'll find it raw."
The leader then put out a new decree
commanding able-bodied men to saw

and store an even greater hoard of wood.
Two weeks went by. The chieftain called again
to ask the weather service if they could
confirm they still foresaw bleak weather when

the winter's force had firmly settled in.
They echoed what they'd told him once before:
"We have no doubt the freeze will soon begin.
We're certain months-long, numbing cold's in store."

The chief insists: "I'd like to know how you
can pledge the coming winter will be bad?"

"The facts are clear," they said. "We're sure it's true,
'cause Indian men are stocking wood like mad."

JUMPING TO CONTUSIONS

PALS AL and Joe who bungee-jump with glee
conceive a clever project one fine day.
Instead of risking blood and guts for free,
they hatch a plan to make their pastime pay.

"You know," says Al, "we'd rake in lots of dough
if we set up a bungee-jumping rig
across the Rio Grande in Mexico.
The splash it generates could turn out big."

Convinced they've got it right, the daring pair
set out at once to pool their funds to shop
for gear that will enable them to share
free-falling flights with those who wish to drop.

They load their truck and trek across the creek,
erecting on a square their enterprise
which draws a crowd that wants to sneak a peek.
In minutes they are ringed with puzzled eyes.

To clarify what they have brought to town
our businessmen decide to demonstrate.
Al dons the harness, mounts the mast, and down
he drops.   On Al's rebound Joe sees his mate

has cuts and scratches on his neck and face.
Joe tries to catch him but to no avail.
Al dives, springs back, but Joe still can't keep pace
and grabs at Al in vain.   The latter's pale;

he's bruised and losing blood.   Since Joe can't seize
him, down goes Al once more, then up he comes.
He's truly damaged now.   Joe mutters, "Geez!
what's going on?"   For once he's not all thumbs

and captures Al, who's worse than borderline.
"Good Lord!   You look bad hurt.   Your head is swelling.

The cord! Was it too long?" "No, that was fine,
but what the hell's "piñata"[14] they keep yelling?"

---

[14] A hanging pot filled with candies and small gifts which is broken with
a stick at a masquerade or children's party.

A LAS SEPTINA DE LA TARDE
or, A Lot of Bull
(A rhyming sestina, sort of...)

HE STRUTTED, arrogant into the ring,
determined, grim, prepared to take a stand.
He'd make his mark; the bull would feel his sting.
He held his flowing, scarlet cape in hand,
alert for what the afternoon would bring.
His little finger bore a golden band.

A *paso doble* blasted from the band.
He focused on his sweetheart's slender ring,
the symbol, she had said, that love would stand
the test of time, although she'd borne the sting
his single-minded quest had called to hand
and anguished over what fierce fate might bring.

So close, so close, olé! He strove to bring
the brute to graze his body as the band
kept trumpeting the action in the ring.
She prayed alone at home; she could not stand
the bull ring's sights. Hot tears of joy would sting
her eyes if only she could stay his hand.

Well, I must say, you've really got to hand
it to the man. He did his best to bring
his skill to bear and mugged to beat the band.
Emboldened when the cheers began to ring,
our ace ignored the bull and turned to stand
and shout, "Hey, ox, you're just an insect's sting!"

The outraged bull, indignant at this sting,
gave raging, throaty snorts, while, hat in hand,
our hero faced the crowd, intent to bring
Madrid's elite up on their feet. The band,
now whipped to frenzy, made the heavens ring
with *paso triples*; players rose to stand.

The bull took aim; he could no longer stand

the taunts. His bovine pride had felt the sting,
and he resolved to launch a hand-to-hand.
He rumbled toward his foe, prepared to bring
a prong to play—henceforth no ploy was banned—
and chased the chastened chump around the ring.

A horn engaged our hero's pants. The ring
of shaken fans, aghast, could hardly stand
the stress. The trousers' rear was rent! A sting!
The point had broken skin! "Come, lend a hand!"
the handlers cried. "Torero down! Quick, bring
a cape to shroud the mooning bum! Play band!"

To bring this tale to end, the shame will stand
a hand above all others; what a sting!
Two rings, an ace disgraced, a loud brass band.

THE YOUNG WIDOW[15]

TO LOSE a mate is sure to prompt much more than sighs.
Heart-wrenching cries arise, but then one finds relief.
At last the blight takes flight on wings of Time, and grief
    Gives way to joys that Time supplies.
    Between a spouse who's borne her loss
    A day and one whose albatross
Has dimmed a year or so there's little common ground;
    One would not take them for the same.
Most people shun the first; the other draws them 'round.

The former breathes real sighs—or plays the sighing game.
She'll sound the self-same theme at every chance she gets:
    Poor girl, she's wholly overwrought.
    They're words she mouths, not pure regrets.
    This tale will show it all means naught
    by shedding light on what is true.
    A beauty's spouse, with dimming view,
Was taking lasting leave, his loved one at his side:
"Beloved, wait; I'll follow, for my soul," she cried,
"Will never part with yours; I'll fly away with you."
    The husband made the trip alone.
The belle's judicious father wisely set the tone:
    He let the flood of tears ensue.
    At last, to raise her hopes anew:
"My child," he said, "it's better that you cease to weep.
The dear departed would not wish for you to steep
Your charms in tears. Embrace the living, not the dead.

    I don't pretend that in a trice
    Conditions will so soon entice
    My daughter to a marriage bed;
But when sufficient time has passed perhaps you'll gaze
With favor on a handsome, young new mate who pays
    You court—quite different from your first." A wail:
    "Ah no. I choose to take the veil."

---

[15] Translated from the fable "*La jeune veuve*" by Jean de La Fontaine
(1621-1695).

At this her father lets her plumb her fall from grace.
  A month of this goes by apace.

Another month brings with it changes every day
In dress, in lingerie, in how she does her hair:
    She mourns at last with stylish air,
    Though not as yet in bright display.
    Her flair returns in full array:
Reluctant laughter, games to play, and songs to sing
    All take their turn as time proceeds.
    In mornings or as day recedes
    she drains deep drafts from Girlhood's spring.
Her father fears the dear departed spouse no more
And thus has ceased to mention it to her, so she
    Inquires at his study door:
    "Where is the mate you promised me?"

Forever wilt thou love, and she be fair!-
"Ode on a Grecian Urn," by John Keats.

LIEBESTOD[16]
(A villanelle)

Supreme for every day these fifty years,
my joy to see her face has never waned,
but time grows short, and with it grow my fears.

It hasn't all been laughter; there've been tears,
though through it all our love has always reigned
supreme for every day these fifty years.

When we were twenty there were no frontiers;
the world was ours, and worries never pained,
but time grows short, and with it haunting fears.

A sickness now holds sway; her torment sears
my soul, but our devotion has remained
supreme for every day these fifty years.

The voice that through the years has thrilled my ears
will soon be stilled; the prospect leaves me drained,
as time grows short for me to face my fears.

The Lord now calls her home; I know she hears.
She'll soon be free of earthly hurt, unchained.
Supreme, she's filled my days these fifty years.
The time's now short, and I must face my fears.

---

[16] Love-death (not autobiographical)

MAGGIE
or
Here Today, Gone Tomorrow

THERE once was a she-cat called Maggie
that Dougie tied up in a baggie.
Stuffed the cat in a pail,
water muffled her wail;
no more will her tail waggie-waggie.

Look! In the Sky! It's a Bird, It's a Plane...No, It's a Bloomin' Pantoum![17]

IT'S TIME once more to pen a pome for Sis;
the months race by so fast it leaves me dazed,
but sure enough, again it's come to this.
All year so far I've sat around and lazed,

but months are racing by and leave me dazed.
I've got to get my act on stage at last;
instead of having sat around and lazed
I should already have some words amassed.

I'll have to get my greetings staged at last
for Joyce's birthday's just around the bend,
and as of now I have no words amassed.
I'm lucky, since it's not too late to send

fond thoughts; her birthday's just around the bend,
thus that is what I plan to do right now.
With any luck I'll still have time to send
best wishes and will thus avoid a row.

So here's a warm embrace; I'll send it now,
since, sure enough, again it's come to this.
BEST WISHES! There, it's done: there'll be no row,
as one more time I pen a pome for Sis.

---

[17] In this poem I have deliberately misspelled the word poem to make sure that it is counted as one syllable

LOVE YA, SWEETIE!

HERSHEY™ chocolate, Tootsie Rolls™,
Milky Ways™, Three Musketeers™,
sugar-frosted flakes in bowls
lead astray our little dears.

What we drink instead of water
makes for vacant, toothless smiles.
Let's be real: we hadn't oughter
yield to Pepsi's™ honeyed wiles.

Frozen popsicles in fridges,
Ben and Jerry's™ ice cream bars,
lead to root canals and bridges,
finance dentists' costly cars.

If we don't escape this trap
we may have to live on pap.

MAYA'S FIRST BIRTHDAY
(The story of a long-distance adoption)

SHE'S TRAVELED far, made quite a pilgrimage
from Haryana half the world around,
a lofty feat at such a tender age,
and now she's home where warmth and love abound.

It wasn't easy, Mom and Dad attest,
much paperwork and many trips abroad,
repeated setbacks, holdups that depressed,
while tension grew and apprehension gnawed.

But when the red light turned to green at last,
long months of hope dissolved in tears of bliss.
An end to looking back, all that is past;
no other joy in life compares to this.

Dear Maya, precious princess, grace and light,
your future beckons, glorious and bright.

PHARMACEUTICALS FOR FOILING PHYSICAL FAILINGS

SUPPOSE pernicious low back pain
begins to cramp creative loafin',
what better way to beat the bane
than popping pills of ibuprofen?

Let's say the ticker starts to twitch,
thus prompting certain discomposure.
The blessed balm to fill the niche
is Quinidex; it offers closure.

You take a spill, a lesion gapes;
your cherished claret stocks are oozing.
Spread Neosporin on the scrapes,
then Band-Aids to assuage the bruising.

There's help to bridle evil bugs
and ease the aches you would short-circuit;
it's clear there is no dearth of drugs
to rid your bod of ills that irk it.

TO A PASSING BEAUTY[18]

A WOMAN, long and slim, in black, majestic grief,
passed by. The clamor from the street assailed my ears.
With ostentatious sweep of hand, quite free of fears,
she raised her hemline, set it swinging, glimpse so brief

of sculpted leg and stately mien, alert, urbane.
And as for me, contorted like a clown, absurd,
I thirsted for the lethal silkiness that purred
within her eyes, fierce skies, where loomed a hurricane.

A lightning bolt…then night!--a fleeting, matchless grace
whose glance aroused in me precipitant rebirth.
Must eons pass before I see again your face?

Remote! Too late! Perhaps not ever more on earth!
I know not where you flee, you don't know where I go,
oh you whom I'd have loved, who knew that it was so!

---

[18] Translated from the poem "*A une passante*" from *Les fleurs du mal: tableaux parisiens* of Charles Baudelaire (1821-1867).

ROME'S BELLS

THEIR clappers' clanging strokes spew forth a rage
of raucous clamor, piercing morning's sleep,
cacophonous assault that sets the stage
for angry oaths by those who'd like to sweep
the bells to hell.

To Sunday's faithful, on the other hand,
concordant chimes betoken calls to prayer
and spur their yearning for the promised land;
they welcome early sun, and on the air
the bells that swell.

Pert pigeons scavenge crumbs from kindly fans;
the peals...or clangor...leave them unimpressed.
They strut and peck in birdish glee at man's
concern to feed them, not at all distressed
by bells that knell.

I stretch and yawn; I know the din won't last.
My yearning's focused on a good repast.
The bells, oh well...

WITCHES' WEEKEND WIND-DOWN

TEEMING turnout—witches' coven—
bubbling pots of boiling brew;
they and guests whose hooves are cloven
share a weekend barbecue.

Corn-fed fare to feed the masses,
sizzling beef on searing coals;
sisters sprawled flat on the…grasses,
post spell-casting: weary souls.

"Pop the cork!" shouts thirsty Kirstie,
"Let's begin the bacchanal.
Fill my goblin goblet firsty.
Come on, Katie, be a doll."

Soon the glasses brim with bubbly;
toasts are offered all around.
Shortly tipsy, all see doubly;
how they babble when unbound!

"Soup's on!" Wobbly, but they're standing;
scramble's on to fill their plates.
Semi-sober, cook is handing
corn bread out. She irrigates

those whose tumblers need renewing.
Silence suddenly descends
as they concentrate on chewing
interspersed with elbow bends.

This goes on till after sunset:
revels worthy of the name.
Food and drink needs? None are unmet.
"Sated coven is our aim!"

Sleep will woo the mob till Monday,
stretched supine to nurse their heads.

Witches never work on Sunday:
they recover in their beds.

THERE OUGHTA BE A LAW

THIS LOVE-thy-neighbor stuff is well and good
if he'll just keep his barking dog indoors;
I've also sought to bear but never could
loquacious back-fence gossip-mouthing bores.

Those menus that you're stuck with when you call,
with music yet, as if you had all day:
I'd like to nail the culprits to the wall
and mock their pleas for mercy when they bray.

I'm waiting for the light to change to green
when all at once I hear a thunder clap.
But no, it's worse: a "music"-loving teen
next lane, his windows wide, is blasting rap.

Let's look at level railroad crossings, too.
With red lights flashing, barriers descend
as freight trains pass, then stop, then back; a brew
to hasten even Job around the bend.

While hitting ninety down the interstate,
conferring with my broker on the phone,
I'm cut off by a gran of eighty-eight
at fifty on her sixties Caddy throne.

The fawning waiter at Chez Greasy Spoon:
"I'm Sid, I recommend the blackened bass."
He hovers, mouths his trite, brown-nosing tune
and then of course forgets to fill my glass.

The doctor's nurse says come at ten to eight.
Up late, no time to eat, I shave and bolt,
then leaf through last year's mags…and wait…and wait.
Next time I'll bring my along my trusty Colt.

Not only irksome humans get my goat.
A feeder for the birds atop a pole
draws squirrels that scarf until their bellies bloat.

I pray that indigestion takes its toll.

Besieged on every side by evil's flame,
distress arrayed, frustration, rancor, rage,
no wonder we short fuses slash and maim
and end our days sedated, in a cage.

"Some 17,500 patients received artificial hip joints recalled by Sulzer Orthopedics, Inc. last month. Physicians race to replace the implants. Recall of faulty devices means some patients need immediate surgery."-January 10, 2001 news report.

THE JOINT IS OUT OF WHACK; O CURSED SPITE, THAT EVER MAN WAS BORN TO SET IT RIGHT![19]

OLD JOINTS wear out, like hips and knees,
until it happens now and then
you have to fork out major fees
to try to make them work again.

It takes a surgeon armed with knives,
employing chisel, clamp, and saw,
the sundry tools with which he strives
to counteract a crippling flaw.

Now ponder how their blood ran cold
when, steel and plastic hips installed,
long lists of patients then were told
their faulty rigs had been recalled!

The remedy's at times ill-starred
when fate has dealt you losing cards.

---

[19] (With apologies to W. Shakespeare .
The time is out of joint; O cursed spite,
that ever I was born to set it right. -Hamlet, I, v, 188)

THE DEVIL'S DICTIONARY

THERE WAS a cool Ambrose named Bierce,
whose cynical barbs airs did pierce.
He and Satan conspired
with words honed and hell-fired
to spear sacred cows something fierce.

MAYBELLE AND RUTHIE AT HOME ON THE RANGE

AREN'T cowboys simply adorable? With their tight jeans
and picturesque wide-brimmed hats,
(often concealing extensive hair loss, they say),
and their darling, needle-toed, high-heeled
alligator—or is it rattlesnake?—skin boots.
Don't you just love 'em, Ruthie dear?

My goodness! They're so good-looking.
But how come they're wearing their hats?
That's what cowboys do, you say?
Indoors? My dad always told my brothers
to remove their hats indoors.
Of course, my brothers aren't cowboys.

And the manly shirts, the top three or four buttons open,
giving us a peek at their chest hair,
a pack of Marlboros in the breast pocket,
one lit, held between the fingers of the right hand
encircling the waist of their lady love
on the dance floor.

"Ah do declare! Yo're purty as a pitcher.
Here, lemme hep you with that there beer can, honey.
Drink up, there's more
where that one come from.
Ya gotta keep up, honey, if ya wanna be
a cowboy's girl.
Way ta go!"

LIKE, DON'T BUG ME, MAN[20]

THE CICADA, stoned on grass
as summer passed,
found his noshing stocks real low
when first snows began to blow;
not a single fly infirm,
not one tasty, squirming worm.
He whined of his shrinking girth
at his neighbor's mound of earth,
nagging nearby ant to lend
grub enough so he could end
belly's growls, hang in instead.
"Don't sweat it, you'll get paid," he said,
"Way before fall's crops are in,
and with interest, cool, win-win."
Sister ant's eyes drill the drone;
altruistic dupe she's not.
"How'd you provide when days were hot?"
There's no way she's lending prone.
"Night and day, to large and small
I rapped loud. Don't get all choked."
"You sang? And reeked of pot you smoked?
Well then, dance now, have a ball!"

---

[20] Freely translated from the fable "*La cigale et la fourmi*" by Jean de La Fontaine (1621-1695).

CULTURE CLASH

THE TRAIN from London's Euston station slow-
ly pulled away. The car was very crowd-
ed as a US soldier went from row
to row of seats, his weary figure bowed.

The only place to sit not occupied
was one adjacent to a pompous la-
dy. From it her small frizzy poodle eyed
the khaki-clad young man who asked, "Ma'am, may

I ease my tired bones there next to you?"
The woman struck a haughty pose and said,
"But what then is my Fifi dear to do?
You Yanks are cheeky, fresh, and poorly bred."

The soldier walked away, but after he
had searched through every car without success,
he once again approached the seat where Fi-
fi lay. "I need a seat. I hate to press

you, Ma'am, but really, I'm plumb tuckered out."
The poodle's owner tossed her head and snapped,
"You people from the States! Without a doubt,
you're rude, you're brash, and should be roundly slapped!"

The soldier said no more. Instead, he seized
poor Fifi by the nape and tossed her through
the open window, after which he eased
into the seat. The apoplectic shrew

flushed red and shrieked, demanding someone come
to help her and to castigate this mons-
ter who had caused her Fifi to succumb.
At last her cries gave rise to this response:

An English gentleman across the aisle
addressed the soldier with an earnest tone.
"Young man, it's true you Yanks are lacking style.

You tend to get things wrong; it's long been known.

"You never use your fork the way you must
when eating, and you're all too blooming rich.
Your cars keep right, not left. But most unjust,
you've now thrown out the wrong offending bitch!"

Don't Buy for Me; Car Too Teeny

BEETLE pilot, nimble, smug,
when you risk it on the road,
low and rounded, trim and snug,
boxed by trucks with heavy load,

better have a grave plot paid
and your testament well planned
just in case a dimpled maid,
SUVing, phone in hand,

veering wildly lane to lane,
unaware of where you're at,
sucking cig and lacking brain,
runs you down and stamps you flat.

Bug nostalgia's sweet indeed
if it doesn't make you bleed.

THE DUBLINERS

THE LONE survivors of a roaring storm, two I-
rish sailors found themselves bedraggled, sodden, on-
ly half alive, adrift. Long hours slipped sloshing by.
They languished, listless, limp, their leaky lifeboat blown

by aimless winds. Then all at once the tars espied
a rusted shipboard lantern lying in the boat.
Aroused, one sailor muttered, as the other eyed
the lamp, "I've heard some tales of these. They often
                                        quote

the time that young Aladdin found a magic one
in which a potent genie lurked. He only had
to rub the lamp a bit, and what he wished got done.
Who knows? We might be just as lucky. Things look
                                        bad."

While hardly hoping to achieve success, the sai-
lor rubbed the grubby lamp with eager strokes, and sure
enough, before the tar's astonished eyes a play-
ful genie did indeed emerge, announcing "You're

a lucky man. I'm so delighted to be free
at last that I'm prepared to grant your slightest wish,
though hark! one treasure only, not the standard three.
But even so, you'll not be bound to live on fish."

At that the thoughtless, thirsty sailor blurted "Make
this bloody ocean into Irish beer! We'll feel
like we're back home." The willing genie said, "Your ache
has deeply touched my heart. Convinced that you are
                                        real-

ly hurting, I shall authorize your wish." He clapped
his hands and disappeared. Their vessel was afloat
on Guiness stout. The second tar, disgusted, snapped:
"Nice going! Now we'll have to pee inside the boat!"

THE BIG BANG
(or, Oh, Is That What That Was?)

THEY SAY the primal seed hung there, suppressed,
a skimpy speck of stony stuff, compressed,
comprising monstrous force not yet expressed,
pent up, aboil, though seemingly at rest.

Then all at once a BLAST!--who could have guessed?--
blew fragments to the north, south, east and west
at speeds one hardly could conceive though pressed,
a bit like stirring up a hornet's nest.

The pieces still rush off with zealous zest,
but those of us who've held on tight are blessed
with Walmarts, central heating, and the rest,
blasé, well fed, and largely unimpressed.

BEQUESTS

GREAT Julius said it as as his lifeblood oozed,
his dimming vision focused on his friend:
"Et tu, Brute?" He had been sore abused.
Thus mighty Caesar's era reached its end.

Enfeebled, Goethe strained to raise his head
as death edged near to fold him into night.
For vision as for lucent thoughts, he pled
with murmured, scarcely sounded words, "More light!"

Consumptive Chekhov, as he breathed his last
from rumpled sheets on which he long had lain,
had this to say, existence ebbing fast,
"It's been a long time since I've had champagne."

With any luck I, too, have still got time
to think up parting words, but mine will rhyme!

BESSIE SEES THE WRINKLED DOG

ONE DAY the sharpei slipped his back yard pen
and wandered off to sniff the 'hood's delights.
He knew he'd made a major error when
to right and left lay only foreign sights.

Perplexed, his corrugated brow became
a field of worried furrows deeply etched.
He really hadn't sought explorer's fame
and now wished nothing more than to be fetched.

On learning that her pooch had fled the coop,
his mistress, loving Bess, expressed distress.
Enlisting neighbors' aid, she led a group
afield and prayed devoutly for success.

The search went on all day, a sharpei diem,
till Bess, relieved, at last was first to see 'im.

BIO OF AUTHOR

Emery L. Campbell writes poetry and short works of fiction and nonfiction. He is a past vice president and long-time member of the Georgia Poetry Society and also belongs to the Utah State Poetry Society, the Southeastern Writers Association, and Georgia Writers, Inc. He contributes a regular column on grammar and usage to the newsletter of the latter organization.

Born in 1927 in Monroe, Wisconsin, Mr. Campbell served as a naval aviator from 1945 to 1950. He subsequently graduated from the University of Wisconsin in June 1952 with a BA in French and spent the following two years as a postgraduate student in France. From 1955 until his retirement in 1992 he was employed as an export sales executive. In this capacity he resided for many years in France, England, and Argentina, as well as in the United States, and traveled widely for business and pleasure.

Since early 1988 Mr. Campbell and his wife, Hettie, a native of the Netherlands, have lived in Lawrenceville, GA. The couple have two grown sons, both of whom reside in the Atlanta area.

AFTERWORD

"I consider it unethical to publish a book which I have not read. Mr. Campbell's work impresses me with the overall quality of the humor as much as with the assured technique and linguistic verve. Mr. Campbell is no mean wordsmith. His typical use of heavy alliteration and chiming vowel sounds recommends itself to my imagination as being most appropriate for this brand of light verse. He is not the doctrinaire who will tell you, "In my poem the message is the only thing that matters!" ... and then you find that his craft is, very simply, bad work ... no assured form, no assured style, no technique. No! What we have here is: good message, good work which exudes astonishing aural imagination. The music and euphony of his verse has a power to linger in the memory with facility and it is one of the functions of good poetry to be memorable. All poetry lovers who derive fun and pleasure from these qualities in the poetry they read shall not regret their investment in this author's light, delightful, hilariously comical verse."

THE PUBLISHER

Printed in the United States
70244LV00002B/1-9

9 780973 330182